PUBLIC PRIVATE
PARTNERSHIP-

PUBLIC PRIVATE PARTNERSHIP-

Lessons from Gujarat for Uttar Pradesh

Palakh Jain

PARTRIDGE

A Penguin Random House Company

To order additional copies of this book, contact
Partridge India
000 800 10062 62
orders.india@partridgepublishing.com

www.partridgepublishing.com/india

Contents

Introduction

Gujarat has long been known as a leader among Indian states in enabling private business to flourish, while Uttar Pradesh is among those at the bottom of the ladder. This paper is intended to capture some lessons from the experience of Gujarat that could be of use to U.P., as the latter attempts to become more business friendly. This will be done primarily by evaluating the Public-Private-Partnership (PPP) projects. Public-Private-Partnership (PPP) provides an opportunity for private sector participation in financing, designing, construction, operation and maintenance of public sector programmes and projects.

Government of Uttar Pradesh (GoUP), the first stable majority government in a long time, wants to establish its credibility with investors through a serious effort to resolve the infrastructure deficit, primarily power and transport. It has prepared a policy framework and guidelines, with a process map for line departments seeking to develop and award PPP projects.

GoUP is already pursuing several PPPs such as the Ganga Expressway ($7.5 billion), 6 linked expressways

($12 billion), public transport ($0.3 billion), general road network development ($3.5 billion), Taj International Airport ($1billion), Kushinagar International Airport ($0.25 billion), and urban rejuvenation of 8 cities ($3 billion). Plans are also under various stages of preparation for encouraging PPPs in sectors like technical education, health and tourism.

This paper would attempt a comparative analysis to identify factors underlying Gujarat's success that could possibly be replicated in UP. It would present arguments as to why particular lessons from Gujarat may or may not be suitable for Uttar Pradesh. This will be done for two sectors namely, power and roads. The rationale for selecting these two sectors is the following: in both these states, power and road sector have attracted maximum investment (after ports in Gujarat).

The paper is organized as follows: Section I tries to explore the domain of Public-Private Partnership (PPP) - need for PPP, the definition, key characteristics etc. Section II describes the methodology of the paper. Section III builds on the idea behind PPP in power and the experience of Gujarat and Uttar Pradesh. Section IV follows the lines of Section II with respect to roads. Section VI concludes the paper by providing the lessons to be learnt from the experience of Gujarat by Uttar Pradesh.

1

Public Private Partnership (PPP)

The traditional functions of a state include law, justice and order. A welfare state has a much-expanded role which includes provision of public utilities like road, power and water supply. The state also provides merit goods such as education and health services that have positive externalities. Under the Constitution of India, it is the federal states that are called upon to shoulder most of these responsibilities. The Government of India has been supplementing the efforts of the State Governments in these welfare functions.

Traditionally, a majority of these have been provided through in-house facilities of government i.e. financed and managed directly by them. However, there exist fiscal problem and inefficiencies state run institutions or enterprises (which are typically highly bureaucratic). Hence, private involvement emerges as an alternative to reduce the sources of inefficiency in public organizations and also, to allow them to respond to market forces and become more competitive.

Public-Private-Partnership (PPP) is one such arrangement which provides an opportunity for private sector participation in financing, designing, construction and operation and maintenance of public sector programmes and projects. Under this arrangement, services are delivered by the private sector (non-profit/ for-profit organizations) while the responsibility for providing the service rests with the government. This arrangement requires the government to either enter into a "contract" with the private partner or pay for the services (reimburse) rendered by the private sector. Contracting prompts a new activity, especially so, when neither the public sector nor the private sector existed to provide the service.

There are three things which generally distinguish PPP from direct provision of services by governments, namely (i) a partnership based on well articulated 'contract' (ii) a long term relationship between the public and private sector (iii) flexibility and responsiveness in decision making. It is argued that PPP leads to improvement in both 'efficiency' and 'effectiveness' in service delivery.

1.1 Definition of PPP

There is no unique definition of PPP in the literature (Fourie & Burger, 1999). Various definitions exist due to difference in the understanding of the terms 'public', 'private', and 'partnership' (Wang, 2000). The most accepted definition of 'public sector' is: organizations/ institutions which are financed by budgetary resources of the government and work directly under the control of government. Similarly, 'private sector' institutions are those, which are not financed by the budgetary resources and are not under the direct control of a government. While defining private sector, some researchers consider non government organizations (NGO) and individuals also as a part of private sector, as these also work outside the direct control of government. Some of the definitions of 'partnership' (e.g. WHO, 1999; Axelsson, Bustreo, & Harding, 2003; World Economic Forum, 2005; Blagescu & Young, 2005) encompass all possible interactions between a government entity and a private player. However, in this context, the most accepted definition of partnership is an agreement between two or more parties to share the responsibilities and reap the gains/losses together in a manner that optimally allocates the risks. As a consequence of wide variations in the understanding of the three terms, a range of definitions of PPP can be identified in the literature.

A project developed on PPP is widely considered to be the project which is developed on an understanding between government and private players to operate and deliver goods/services with sufficient risk being transferred to private players (Mitchell-Wever et al,

1991; Kolzow, 1994; Corry, 1997). The transfer of risk is the most important element as it ensures managerial efficiency (x-efficiency) and also helps avoid moral hazard. Government of India (GoI) has defined a PPP project as "a project based on a contract or concession agreement, between a government or statutory entity on the one side and a private sector company on the other side, for delivering an infrastructure service on payment of user charges" (Department of Economic Affairs - Ministry of Finance, Government of India and ADB, 2006). The term 'payment of user charges' in the definition indicates transfer of revenue risk to the private sector. Technically, any project which harnesses resources from both the public and private sector is a PPP, but a narrower and more formal definition entails that the project have at least a 51% private component.

According to Planning Commission, PPP is a mode of implementing government programmes/schemes in partnership with the private sector. The term private in PPP encompasses all non-government agencies such as the corporate sector, voluntary organizations, self-help groups, partnership firms, individuals and community based organizations, PPP, moreover, subsumes all the objectives of the service being provided earlier by the government, and is not intended to compromise on them. Essentially, the shift in emphasis is from delivering services directly, to service management and coordination. The roles and responsibilities of the partners may vary from sector to sector. While in some schemes/projects, the private provider may have significant involvement in regard to all aspects of implementation; in others s/he may have only a minor role.

Some researchers and policy makers consider PPP and Private Finance Initiative (PFI) as synonymous. In PFI, government purchases only service and no assets. Thus, PFI should be considered as a special case of PPP.

1.2 Costs and Benefits associated with PPP

Public Private Partnership (PPP) has become a preferred method, across both developed and developing countries for infrastructure development due to its inherent advantages over other methods, in the recent years (Department of Economic Affairs - Ministry of Finance, Government of India & ADB, 2006). Some of the advantages identified in the literature are managerial efficiency gain, modern techniques of management though right set of stakeholders, high-end technological input, process efficiency, improved service response, rigorous risk appraisal and optimal risk allocation among various players, and access to private finance to reduce budgetary constraints. These benefits are derived mainly from efficiency improvements in asset creation and asset management and efficiency and effectiveness improvements in service delivery.

Some other potential **benefits** expected from PPP are:

1 Cost-effectiveness-The selection of the developer/ service provider depends on competition or some bench marking, the project is generally more cost effective than otherwise.

2 Higher Productivity- By linking payments to performance, productivity gains may be expected within the programme/project.

3 Accelerated Delivery –The contracts generally have incentive and penalty clauses vis-a-vis implementation of capital projects/programmes. This leads to accelerated delivery of projects.

4 Clear Customer Focus - The shift in focus from service inputs to outputs create the scope for innovation in service delivery and enhances customer satisfaction.

5 Recovery of User Charges- Innovative decisions can be taken with greater flexibility on account of decentralization. Wherever possibilities of recovering user charges exist, the same can be imposed in harmony with local conditions.

However, certain characteristics of infrastructure projects make them unattractive to private investors. Their long gestation periods increase the uncertainty of investments and the risk of non-recovery of the initial capital expenditure. On the other hand, it is not possible for the government to single-handedly raise all the necessary funds for infrastructure development In addition, the operation and maintenance of public amenities like roads and airports does not form a part of the core functions of the government. These assets would be much more efficiently managed in the hands of competent private parties.

1.3 PPP and Privatization

PPP involves a long-term relationship between the public sector and the private sector. While the collaboration between the two, may take various forms like buyer-seller relationship, donor-recipient relationship, the most stable partnership is in the form of 'contract' binding on both the parties. The following are the main differences between public-private-partnership and 'privatization':

a). **Responsibility**: Under privatization the responsibility for delivery and funding a particular service rests with the private sector. PPP, on the other hand, involves full retention of responsibility by the government for providing the service.

b). **Ownership**: While ownership rights under privatization are sold to the private sector along with associated benefits and costs, PPP may continue to retain the legal ownership of assets by the public sector.

c). **Nature of Service**: While nature and scope of service under privatization is determined by the private provider, under PPP the nature and scope of service is contractually determined between the two parties.

d). **Risk and Reward**: Under privatization all the risks inherent in the business rest with the private sector. Under PPP, risks and rewards are shared between the government (public) and the private sector.

2

Methodology

The experiences of PPP can be analyzed by examining individual projects in the two sectors to arrive at the lessons useful for Uttar Pradesh from the experience of Gujarat. These issues can be assimilated across sectors to understand the implications and policy issues for increasing the role of PPP in Uttar Pradesh. The paper is based on the analyses of projects in power and roads. The rationale for selection of these projects has been laid out in the introduction section. Selection of projects has been based on the availability of information regarding a project. Data/information regarding individual projects used in this paper has been collected from secondary sources (viz. case studies, research papers, working papers, reports, published policy guidelines, and various government websites). Primary data is collected via interactions with government officials.

The paper first defines PPP based on various definitions in the existing literature. Thereafter, individual projects in the two sectors (Power and roads) are analyzed. The lessons are drawn by collating the analysis done for these two sectors.

Individual project can be studied by analyzing the two stages (formation stage and implementation stage) of a PPP project. Each of these stages is identified with a set of phases of the project. Formation stage of PPP is identified with initiative (idea) phase, definition phase, bidding, and a part of design phase. The design phase part may just have a discussion on the type of structures and shape. The engineering design is developed in the next stage only. In this stage, the project takes a shape and a concrete deliverable is defined for the private developer. Most often, informal discussions with various prospective private parties are also carried out. These discussions help in shaping the project in such a way so as to unlock maximum value from the project. Realization stage consists of engineering design, working design, construction phase, rehabilitation phase, operation phase, and maintenance phase of a project. This is a relatively larger stage. In this stage, once the project becomes operational, the outputs (benefits) are reaped over the years. Figure 1 shows the two stages of a PPP project and corresponding phases of the project.

As discussed above individual projects can be studied in the two stages for each of the sectors. The rationale for carrying out the two stage analysis is that the experiences in the two stages may be different. The experiences in the formation stage are mostly process related experiences. Formation stage faces a challenge of conceiving a project in a manner that the outcome is not very different from what was desired. At the same time, the project needs to be planned to unlock maximum value from the private player apart from being viable on its own or creating minimum burden on the government resources, as the case may be. Selection of right private stakeholders is also a complex process. Realization stage experiences are mainly outcome related experience, which is equally complex. This stage faces challenges like land acquisition, design complexities, operation related issues, and environmental & social concerns. There are also threats from other competing projects, which might come up in the vicinity and affect the viability of the existing project. Thus, the experiences in the two stages are different Hence; the issues arising out of the two stages are different from each other.

Analyses of the experiences in the formation stage will help in identifying issues mainly related to the process, which is followed for the development of the projects on PPP. Analysis of experiences in realization stage will be helpful in identifying issues mainly related to the outcome of a PPP project. However, there will be some process related issues in this stage as well.

The above is an ideal way of analyzing a PPP project. However, due to paucity of data and confidentiality of contracts, the same is not possible. Hence, in the paper the lessons will be drawn at a macro level e.g. institutional framework and policy issues.

3

Power

3.1 Indian Scenario

India has the fifth largest electricity generation capacity in the world. The majority of generation, transmission and distribution capacities are with either public sector companies or with State Electricity Boards (SEBs). The broad policy framework in place is as per the Electricity Act 2003 and National Electricity Policy 2005. In power sector, there are independent Regulators: Central Electricity Regulatory Commission for Central PSUs and inter-State issues. Each State has its own Electricity Regulatory Commission.

The private sector participation is increasing especially in generation and distribution. Distribution licenses for several cities are already with the private sector and many large generation projects have been planned in the private sector. GoI has allowed 100% FDI in Generation, Transmission and Distribution - the Government is keen to draw private investment into the sector. GoI is also trying to lure the private sector by offering incentives like Income tax holiday for a block of 10 years in the first 15 years of operation and waiver of capital goods import duties on mega power projects (above 1,000 MW generation capacity).

So far, there have been two PPP projects in power sector. These include Tala (transmission) and Delhi Discom (distribution). One upcoming PPP is Tata-DVC (generation). However, there has not been any PPP in power sector in Gujarat and UP.

3.2 Gujarat

Though Gujarat has not initiated any PPP in its power sector, Gujarat has achieved its place in upper level of the best users of Electricity in almost all walks of life. The overall experience of Gujarat can be evaluated to draw lessons for Uttar Pradesh.

The per capita electrical energy consumption in Gujarat was 944 units during 2002-03 which is much higher than that of National average. The Government of Gujarat enacted the Gujarat Electricity Industry (Reorganisation & Regulation) Act in May 2003. This act aimed to provide for reorganisation and rationalisation of electricity industry in the state and for establishing an Electricity Regulatory Commission in the state for regulating the electricity industry and all other in related aspects. The salient features of the Act are as under:

- Reorganization of the Gujarat Electricity Board.
- Empowering state regulator to become nodal agency for regulating the industry in Gujarat, determining tariff, wheeling charges, surcharge etc.
- Defining role of State Government
- Aligning tariffs towards cost of supply.

The current electricity demand in the Gujarat State is on an average of the order of 9000 MW. The maximum demand catered and the installed capacity is less than this figure. An assessment of the power demand requirements for the State over the time horizon FY2000-FY2010 indicates the following build-up:

3.2.1 Notable points from Gujarat's power sector

Gujarat is leading other states in taking benefits of the provisions of Electricity Act, 2003. If the efforts are made in the right direction, the state can reap the benefits of the first mover advantage. With respect to the regulatory support, Gujarat is one of the first states to appoint a fully independent and functional regulator for the electricity sector. The Gujarat Electricity Regulatory Commission (GERC) became functional from 2000. It has issued a tariff order in the year 2000 and 2004. The Commission has already indicated its inclination for setting market mechanism in the State of Gujarat. GERC is the sole licensing authority for transmission, distribution and trading. It has also initiated efforts for determination of tariffs, charges and surcharges, etc. This would create and promote necessary infrastructure for bringing about competition driven efficiencies in the sector leading to opening up of investments opportunities in the sector. Other initiatives of this sector to achieve the objective of sectoral reforms are: adoption of professional management techniques for the newly formed entities, implementation of distribution franchisee framework to expedite commercial improvements and outsourcing of commercial activities like metering, billing and collection in distribution.

4

Roads

4.1 Indian Scenario

Provision of quality road network is a pre-requisite for the economy to achieve a higher growth trajectory on a sustained basis. The importance of transport cannot be ignored. A well laid out road network is essential for efficient and cost effective movement of men and goods, without which trade and industry cannot maintain a competitive edge. Road infrastructure is absolutely critical for the Indian economy. There has been a tremendous increase in the share of road transportation vis a vis rail over the last four decades with the total freight movement increasing from 11% to 60% and the passenger movement from 26% to 80%. In other words, our economy which was earlier rail dominated, has now become predominantly road dominated (Gujarat Infrastructure Development Board).

The road network in the country consists of National Highways (which constitute 2% of India's road network, and carry approximately 40% of the total traffic volume, providing connectivity between the major economic hubs), State Highways (which connect the State capital with the various district centers, other important cities, towns and minor ports within a State, and also provide connectivity to the National Highways), District Roads (which facilitate local trade by connecting production centers with the markets and the highways and railway stations), Village Roads and Municipal Roads. The Central Government is responsible for the development and maintenance of National Highways under the National Highways Act, 1956. The National Highways Authority of India was constituted by an act of Parliament, the National Highways Authority of India Act, 1988. It is responsible for the development, maintenance and management of National Highways entrusted to it and for matters connected or incidental thereto. The authority was operationalised in February; 1995.The Ministry of Road Transport and Highways (MoRT&H) is the coordinating agency responsible for planning, technical standardization and budgeting for National Highways, on behalf of the Central Government. The respective State Governments are mandated with the development and maintenance of all roads other than the National Highways (Gujarat Infrastructure Development Board).

4.2 Roads Sector: Uttar Pradesh

Uttar Pradesh is a landlocked state. Thus it is the road sector that caters to the needs of the expanding demand for transport facilities due to the explosive growth in the number of vehicles on account of non-availability of adequate public/goods transport facilities. The government has therefore enhanced its focus on roads since the Tenth Five Year Plan in spite of the resource crunch faced by it. However, despite the government's efforts, only 40 per cent of state highways and 4 per cent of major district roads are two-laned. More than one-third of the roads in Uttar Pradesh are unsurfaced and almost half of the unsurfaced roads are non-motorable. In addition, about 36 per cent of state highways are below the standard single-lane roads.

4.2.1 Overview

- The total road network in the state is 229,265 km.
- On the policy front an important development has been the formulation of the State Road Policy in 1998. The basic purpose of the policy was to lay down proper and well-defined strategies for the development of roads.
- In 1999, the state government framed guidelines to encourage private participation in roads and bridges projects on BOT basis. The UP State Bridge Corporation was made the nodal agency

for such projects. However, despite this, private participation in the state is negligible.

- The major road schemes in the state are funded by the CRF, Nabard and the World Bank.

4.2.2 National Highways

The state has a total of 4,931 km of national highways. Thirty-five national highways pass through the state. These are NH-2, NH-2A, NH-3, NH-7, NH-12A, NH-19, NH-24, NH-24A, NH-25, NH-25A, NH-26, NH-27, NH-28, NH-28B, NH-28C, NH-29, NH-56, NH-56A, NH-56B, NH-58, NH-72A, NH-73, NH-74, NH-75, NH-76, NH-86, NH-87, NH-91, NH-91A, NH-92, NH-93, NH-96, NH-97 and NH-119. Of the total length, 1,952.84 km is being upgraded by NHAI under the first three phases of the NHDP (until November 2006). Only 235 km has been completed under the NHDP as of November 2006 (NHAI).

4.2.3 Road Works at the State Level

The total planned expenditure incurred in the state on roads and bridges in 2005-06 amounted to Rs 14.72 billion. The total non-planned expenditure incurred during the year was Rs 12.01 billion. Of the non-planned expenditure, CRF expenditure amounted to Rs 3.16 billion and maintenance expenditure amounted to Rs 8.85 billion. In July 2006, MSRTH approved 17 road improvement proposals under the CRF at a cost of Rs 1.83 billion.The outlay for 2006-07 was Rs 23.83 billion including an outlay of Rs 2.91 billion for RIDF and Rs 5 billion for World Bank-aided State Road Project II.

4.2.3.1 World Bank-funded State Road project II

The World Bank-aided State Road Project was approved in 2002 and involves upgradation and rehabilitation of over 3,300 km of roads. The total estimated cost of the project is Rs 29.52 billion of which Rs 23.42 billion has been made available by the World Bank. The rest of the cost is being borne by the state government. The project is divided into two phases – Phase I involving upgradation of 397 km and rehabilitation of 808 km and Phase II involving rehabilitation of 2,100 km in addition to construction of four bypasses and five major bridges.Under Phase I, upgradation works for 397 km in four packages are in progress. All maintenance works under Phase I have been completed. Works under Phase II are in progress under 29 packages. The entire project is expected to be completed by December 2008.

4.2.3.2 Private Projects

The state government has not been successful in attracting private participation in road projects. In 1999, the state government framed guidelines to encourage private participation in roads and bridges projects on BOT basis. The UP State Bridge Corporation was made the nodal agency for such projects. However, only one major bridge over the river Sone in Chopan was constructed by the corporation on BOT basis. Private participation could not take off mainly on account of frequent changes of government in the state.

To encourage private participation, the state government has identified about 20 highly commercial and viable ROBs (with a financial rate of return of over 20 per cent) for construction on BOT basis. In addition, the UP State Highway Authority has also identified nine state highways (1,265 km) for upgradation, six state highways (504 km) for maintenance and construction of another six ROBs on BOT basis. The necessary action has been initiated for the appointment of consultants for the required survey and preparation of the project report and bid documents. Meanwhile, a toll policy is also being worked on. Feedback Ventures gave its report on a toll policy for the state. However, in May 2005, the government asked for a revised report on the policy which is yet to be finalized.

4.2.3.3 Nabard-Assisted Projects

During 2005-06, 1,055 road works of 1,468 km length and costing Rs 2.04 billion were sanctioned under Nabard. Of these, 27 road works and 15 bridges were completed by September 2005. For 2006-07, an outlay of Rs 2.91 billion was proposed which included Rs 500 million for district roads. As per the tenth plan target,

216 bridges were to be constructed during the plan period. Of these, 96 bridges, including 65 under the Nabard scheme were completed by March 2005 and 15 another bridges by September 2005.

4.2.3.4 Pradhan Mantri Gram Sadak Yojana (PMGSY)

As can be seen from the table below, Uttar Pradesh has performed well in the first three phases of the PMGSY, achieving the average performance ratio. However, the state is way below the average performance mark for the fourth phase. While under Phase IV no works have been completed, under Phase V, no works have been sanctioned under the project.

4.2.4 Maintenance Works

Funds for maintenance are provided through the state budget. However, since these funds were not adequate, the state government created a separate state road fund by imposing an additional trade tax on sale of diesel and petrol. During 2005-06, funds available under the state road fund and annual maintenance were Rs 6.3 billion and Rs 1.2 billion respectively. In 2004-05, Rs 4.79 billion was made available under the state road fund and Rs 1.20 billion under annual maintenance against which the expenditure was Rs 4.14 billion and Rs 1.16 billion respectively.

4.2.5 Looking Forward

In terms of investment, the state claims to spend Rs 10 billion annually on the road sector. However, the actual amount spent is much lower. Sufficient funds have not been allocated to maintenance of roads and whatever funds were allocated in the past were diverted to network expansion. The recent expansion of the road network in Uttar Pradesh has been mainly in other district roads or the village roads. However, road conditions continue to remain poor. The state does not fare well in terms of road density compared to national numbers. Moreover, the comparison turns worse "if only surfaced and motorable unsurfaced roads are taken into account".

There is a need for the state to focus more on private participation both for speedier implementation of projects and for bringing about efficiency. The state's BOT policy guidelines are not well thought out. In contrast, states such as Gujarat, Madhya Pradesh and Andhra Pradesh have policies that clearly define how risks are going to be shared between a private developer and the state government and also enumerate incentives provided to private sector participants. Thus, fundamental changes are required in the way the government manages and finances the road network.

4.3 Gujarat

Gujarat has 18,286 km of state highways, 37,315 km of district roads and 49,150 km of rural roads. Even though the existing road network in Gujarat is qualitatively rated as the best in the country, it is grossly insufficient, and is in need of major up gradation and improvement in order to meet with the present transportation needs. Recognizing this fact, Government of Gujarat has decided to accord special priority to road development and to revamp the road policy with a view to effectively meet with the challenging task ahead. Involvement of private sector is one of the steps.

Gujarat is one of the few states in the country to have proactively developed its road sector. The total road length in the state has increased tenfold since 1947. Its current road network is 102,071 km. Over 85 per cent of the road length in the state has bituminous surfacing. The state government has been successful in mobilizing funds from various sources such as the central government, budgetary sources, multilateral agencies and the private sector.

Over the last 10 years, the state has set many benchmarks and accounts for several firsts in the road development arena. It has to its credit the first expressway of the country 惆 the Ahmedabad-Vadodara expressway (NE-I). It is also amongst the first few states to attract private sector participation in road projects and developed the

Ahmedabad-Mehsana and Vadodara-Halol toll roads through private sector participation. Gujarat, through the Gujarat Infrastructure Development Act, 1999, was the first state to implement a law governing BOT transactions and other such arrangements. The state has also formed a wholly owned government undertaking, the Gujarat State Road Development Corporation (GSRDC), to implement the road development plans laid down in the agenda. The state has forecasted traffic growth up to 2017. The details of this forecast are given in the table below.

4.3.1 National Highways

The state has a total of 3,260 km of national highways. Eleven national highways and one expressway passes through the state. These are NH-6, NH-8, NH-8A, NH-8B, NH-8C, NH-8D, NH-8E, NH-14, NH-15, NH-59, NH-113 and NE-1.Of the total length of national highways, 1,365.66 km is being upgraded by NHAI under the first five phases of the NHDP (until November 2006). A total of 637.06 km has already been completed (India Infrastructure). The details of the same are given in Table AA. Apart from the NHDP, MSRTH has also completed four projects covering 18.9 km at a total cost of Rs 2.13 billion on BOT (toll) basis.

Roads are being developed by the initiative of the Roads and Buildings Department of Gujarat, GSRDC, and the Gujarat Infrastructure Development Board (GIDB) as well as through the CRF and Nabard funds.

4.3.2 Public Sector Road Projects

4.3.2.1 Central Road Fund (CRF)

CRF sanctions are provided to develop both state roads and village roads. Till December 2006, works covering 6,344.18 km requiring an investment of Rs 57.15 billion had been sanctioned. Of the total works, 495 works covering 5,117.96 km have been completed. Around Rs 43 billion was received by the state from the CRF, of which it has spent Rs 37 billion.

4.3.2.2 Gujarat State Highways Project

The World Bank-assisted project is being implemented by the Roads and Buildings Department. The project was initiated in 2000 to enhance the capacity of the Gujarat government to effectively and efficiently plan and manage state road infrastructure as well as maximize the asset utilization of the existing road infrastructure. The total cost of the project is $533 million, of which the World Bank is contributing $381 million. The World Bank had disbursed $241.24 million till June 2006. The project implementation period is five years and the loan repayment period is 20 years. The project includes widening and strengthening of about 850 km of state highways and periodic maintenance of around 1,000 km of state highways. The widening and strengthening component is being implemented in three phases — Phase I (247.31 km), Phase IIA (240.62 km) and Phase IIB (368.45 km). While Phase I and Phase IIA works are complete, Phase IIB works are under implementation. The details of the works are given in the Table BB. According to the World Bank, project progress is on track. The Roads and Buildings Department's capacity for effective management of the state road network, particularly in policy, planning, project management, monitoring and reporting functions, has been substantially strengthened. The completion of around 1,250 km of works has resulted in an increase in travel speed by 20-30 per cent and reduction of transport cost by about 10 per cent.

4.3.2.3 Gujarat Emergency Earthquake Rehabilitation Project

This project comprises rehabilitation work in earthquake-affected districts, strengthening of roads and reconstruction and repair of bridges affected due to the earthquake in 2001. The major work under this project has been completed with assistance from the World Bank, ADB and the Gujarat State Disaster Management Authority. The details of this project are given below.

4.3.3 Private Sector Projects

Gujarat was the first state in India to enact legislation on infrastructure development, namely, the Gujarat Infrastructure Development Act, 1999. The state government had earlier set up the Gujarat Infrastructure Development Board in 1995 which facilitates the flow of funds from the private sector into the infrastructure sectors and also ensures coordination amongst various agencies. The state has also amended its Motor Vehicles Taxation Act, 1951 to enable levying of tolls.

The private sector has made a total investment of around Rs 6 billion in the road sector. Though Gujarat was one of the leading states to promote PPP in road development, the involvement of the private sector has decreased considerably over the years. While the private sector has completed four projects at a total cost of Rs 4.96 billion, the remaining four projects under implementation have a total investment of only Rs 0.89 billion. Two of the most noteworthy PPP projects are the Ahmedabad-Mehsana Toll Road (completed at a cost of Rs 3 billion) and the Vadodara-Halol Toll Road (completed at a cost of Rs 1.61 billion). Both these roads were developed by SPVs — Ahmedabad-Mehasana Toll Road Company Limited (formed by L&T) and Vadodara-Halol Toll Road Company Limited (formed by IL&FS) respectively. These SPVs are JVs of the state government and IL&FS. The two SPVs have recently been merged into a single company called Gujarat Toll Road Investment Company Limited. The GSRDC has five PPP projects in its portfolio. However, these are very small projects involving a cumulative investment of only about Rs 1.16 billion. Table CC gives details of private sector projects in Gujarat.

4.3.3.1 World Bank assisted Gujarat Rural Roads Project

The State Government has recently successfully completed a Rs.350.00 crores World Bank Assisted Rural Road Project. Under this, about 6100 kms of new construction/reconstruction and improvement of rural roads have been completed in 13 out of 19 districts in the state. This is probably the most successful World Bank assisted Road Project in the country to date.

4.3.4 Gujarat's Road Sector: A sum up

The projects remaining to be taken up by the state government which fall under the 2020 plan are given in Table DD. Overall, the progress in the state looks quite positive. Road density in the state stands at 53.72 km per 100 square km as against the national average of 77 km. The state government has taken a policy decision to give priority to road development in the future. It has formulated an infrastructure development plan, the "Gujarat Infrastructure Agenda – Vision 2010." Under this, road development expenditure will account for

17.05 per cent (Rs 199.51 billion) of the total planned investment.

Despite these initiatives, the magnitude of private investment remains low in terms of value (Rs 6 billion) as compared to certain other states such as Maharashtra (Rs 150 billion) and Rajasthan (Rs 29 billion). The state government thus needs to ramp up its initiative to promote private sector participation in road development.

A. POLICY FRAMEWORK

A.1 **Vision Document**: A clear policy advocating the rationale of PPPs provides political commitment and support for the program. This is vital particularly in the initial years of a PPP program. Gujarat realized the importance of formulating such a policy and prepared Vision document. Each government department in Gujarat is seen to work towards the objectives laid down in the Vision Document. This document provides clarity on other aspects, such as the approach towards risk transfer, procurement, financing, and the need for transparency. Setting a policy objective has also encouraged the discussion of key issues among different stakeholders. This can be replicated by U.P.

A.2. **Government's Approach**: Private players need incentives to embark on a PPP project. It is essential for the government to be investor friendly and incentivize the private players adequately to attract them. Gujarat has been able to attract funds from private players by converting the unattractive projects into financially viable projects for the private players. In one of the PPP projects where the toll collection was not sufficient due to less traffic, the government of Gujarat gave the toll collection rights of some other roads to attract the private player. Various ways are adopted by Gujarat government to make the projects financially attractive to the private players. Such innovative solutions need to be devised by the government of Uttar Pradesh.

Further, the overall culture of the state plays an important role in attracting the private players. In Gujarat, the acceptance level of private projects in high. This is in contrast to Uttar Pradesh where because of the hostile environment and lack of acceptance by public, the PPP projects have not taken off.

A.3. Policy Relaxations: To reap the maximum from a PPP project, it becomes imperative for the government to relax the rigid policies which may be acting as a barrier for PPP. Gujarat has done the same from time to time. Apart from the policy changes mentioned in the earlier sections, some of the enabling policy changes with regard to PPP projects are:

- Modification in the Urban Land Ceiling Act
- Relative ease of transfer of agricultural land to non-agricultural land

- Rationalization of stamp duties

These relaxations in policies have eased the administrative complications to a great extent and have been an important reason for success of PPP projects in Gujarat.

A.4. Government's role in facilitating markets: Gujarat government has been at the forefront in facilitating the role of markets. The same is needed for success of PPP projects. An example of the same is in the case of 'Land Market Policy'. Unlike other states such as West Bengal, Gujarat government does not act as an intermediary in the process of sale and purchase of land by a farmer to a private player. Hence, the state plays no role in imposing a monopoly or a monopsony price on the value of land. This not only lends transparency but also facilitates growth of markets. This change in role of government from a regulator to a facilitator should be replicated by other states.

A.5 Viability Gap Funding: The Viability Gap Funding(VGF) Scheme of the Government of India provides financial support in the form of grants, one time or deferred, to infrastructure projects undertaken through public private partnerships with a view to make them commercially viable. The Scheme is administered by the Ministry of Finance. Viability Gap Funding under the Scheme is normally in the form of a capital grant at the stage of project construction.

Gujarat government has set up its own VGF. This is a landmark step. Under this scheme, the state government can provide up to 40% of the funding. Even the state of Rajasthan has set up a state VGF for social sector projects. This option may not be viable for a state which is undergoing a fiscal crunch. However, setting up of state VGF should be one of the targets of U.P government to make a mark in the field of PPP.

The following table sums up the policy framework:

B. LEGAL FRAMEWORK

Internationally although not all countries have developed specific new PPP legislation, nearly all have felt it necessary to amend existing legislation. Ireland passed the State Authorities (PPP Arrangements) Act in 2002 which defined the possible range of PPPs that State Authorities could enter into, as well as the role of the Minister of Finance in providing directions to ministries aiming to enter into PPPs (World Bank,2006).

In general, old laws were enacted without PPPs in mind. Gujarat government recognized the same. Legislation can also create new institutions which will play a key role in the PPP process. The details of the institutional framework will be dealt in the next point. The Gujarat government has set up a broad legal framework for PPPs. The same is absent in case of Uttar Pradesh.

Even where legislation is not strictly needed to permit PPPs, it can be helpful in a number of ways. A new legislative framework can for example define and limit the processes used in identifying and procuring PPPs.

According to World Bank report on PPP (2006), consideration should be given to the development of cross-cutting PPP legislation. The legislation already passed by Gujarat, Andhra Pradesh and Punjab provides possible models for other states such as Uttar Pradesh. One important aspect that could be addressed by such legislation is mechanisms for dispute resolution. The development and passage of legislation also allows for consultation and open debate about the government's policy for pursuing PPPs, including the expected benefits and rationale. This could be an important mechanism to help increase the public legitimacy of PPPs.

C. HUMAN RESOURCES

The public sector needs individual capacities to be strengthened to provide the gamut of skills required for an effective PPP program. It requires not just transactions skills, but also those involved in selecting which projects to be pursued as PPPs, estimating the fiscal costs of PPPs, oversight and contract management and ex-post evaluation and auditing of the performance of PPPs. Given public sector pay scales it may be difficult to attract skilled individuals in from the private sector. Consultants can play a large role in providing specialist skills for public authorities in any PPP program. But certain core skills have to remain with the public sector. (World Bank, 2006). One solution is to have quality transaction management services from qualified firms having skills and experience to provide both commercial/financial and legal services in support of PPP transactions. This can help the Sponsoring Authorities make implementation of PPP projects much smoother and efficient.

The Government of Gujarat has pre-qualified a panel of firms through International Competitive Bidding. The shortlisted consultants have been evaluated for their capability and experience in discharging a lead role in PPP transactions. Government of Gujarat has recognized that consultants can play a large role in providing specialist skills for public authorities in any PPP program. At the same time, it has also retained certain core skills with the public sector to make the best use of the consultants.

The Government of Uttar Pradesh is at the same time struggling to get the desired human resource required for an efficient working of the PPP initiatives. The same is attributable in part to the existing bureaucracy in the state and to the widespread corruption in the state economy.

D. STANDARDIZATION OF CONTRACTS, PROCEDURES AND GUIDELINES

Guidelines are often developed which provide specific rules on how projects are to be selected for pursuit through PPPs, on contract design and procurement, and on contract management. These can help ensure that issues such as affordability of the PPP to the government, value-for-money and overall fiscal costs. Further, public legitimacy concerns are addressed properly.

The standardization of common contractual procedures is recommended as it firms up an acceptable public sector risk profile and creates certainty in the market for private players. It can also promote a common understanding of the technical, operational and financial risks that are typically encountered in PPPs. Further, it aids in understanding how such risks should be allocated or shared. A standardization of guidelines provides a consistent approach to risk transfer, risk sharing and value for money across PPPs falling in the same sector, and a reduction in time and cost of negotiations.

There have been some efforts by state governments to develop standard contracts. At the state level, Gujarat and Andhra Pradesh have developed cross-sectoral model contracts. Madhya Pradesh has developed some standard documents in the road sector. At the central level, NHAI has developed model contracts and standard documents for the road sector. Gujarat is one of the pioneering states to have project preparation guidelines and standard documents.

E. INFORMATION DISSEMINATION

There is relatively little information on PPPs in the public domain. This includes examples of contracts and clauses, and assessments of the success of different approaches both in terms of contracting structures as well as institutional frameworks for PPPs. Gujarat is far ahead of most of the Indian states in this regard. Uttar Pradesh lags miserably in this aspect. The latter has not even developed a website to disseminate the basic information about PPPs.

Further, in terms of formalized individual capacity building, the number of specialized courses offered on PPPs in India has been limited. There are some training programs at central or state level, as well as those organized industry organizations such as Confederation of Indian Industry (CII). Many of the government organizations – both at the senior levels and middle levels – take part in these programs. However, with civil servant staff in general shifting position every few years, most of the training imparted can be quickly lost (World Bank,2006).

The following table sums up the broad points of comparison across the two states.

Gujarat's experience offers a plethora of lessons to be learnt by a state like Uttar Pradesh. The existing gaps in the two states with respect to PPP should not be surprising. This is so, in part because U.P government is at an early stage in the development of their PPP programs. Nonetheless it is important that the right frameworks and capacities are further developed in the state.

References

Asthana S, Sue R, and Halliday J (2002). *Partnership Working in Public Policy Provision: A Framework for Evaluation.* Social Policy & Administration, 36 (7), 780-795.

Axelsson H, Bustreo F, Harding A (2003). *Private Sector Participation in Child Health: A Review of World Bank Projects, 1993-2002.* The World Bank, Washington DC.

Blagescu M, Young J (2005). *Partnership and Accountability: Current Thinking and Approaches among Agencies Supporting Civil Society Organizations.* Working Paper 255. Overseas Development Institute, London.

Corry D (1997 Ed). *Public Expenditure: Effective Management and Control.* Th Dryden Press, London

Data, Retrieved on 19 August,2008 from www.gidb.org Data Retrieved on 25 July 2008, http://www.pppinindia.com/

Department of Economic Affairs - Ministry of Finance, Government of India and ADB (2006). *Facilitating*

Public–Private Partnership for Accelerated Infrastructure Development in India. Workshop Report, ADB, New Delhi.

Department of Economic Affairs - Ministry of Finance, Government of India (2007). *Public–Private Partnership-Creating an Enabling Environment for State Projects.*

Fourie F C N & Burger P (1999). *An Economic and Fiscal Analysis and Assessment of PPPs. Unpublished Report of Department of Finance Pretoria.*

Infrastructure, Retrieved on June 22, 2008 from www.infrastructure.gov.in

Investment Commission of India, Retrieved on July 29, 2008 from http://www.investmentcommission.in

Kolzow D R (1994). *Public Private Partnerships: The Economic Development of Organization of the 90s.* Economic Development Review, 12 (1).

Martin D, Moon D, Collings S, and Lewis A (1995). *Mechanisms for Improved Energy Efficiency in Transport.* Overseas Development Administration, London UK

NHAI Data Retrieved on 13 July,2008 from www.gidb.org

Private Participation in Infrastructure database, World Bank, retrieved from http://www.ilfsindia.com/downloads/bus_concept/demystifying_ppp.pdf

Wang Y (2000). *Public Private Partnership in Social Sector: Issues and Country Experiences in Asia and the Pacific.* ADBI Policy Paper No. 1, ADBI, Tokyo, Japan.

World Bank (2006). *India- Building Capacities for Public Private Partnership*

WHO (1999). *WHO Guidelines on Collaborations and Partnership with Commercial Enterprise.* WHO, Geneva.

World Economic Forum (2005). *Building on Monterrey Consensus: The Growing Role of Public Private Partnership in Mobilizing Resources for Development.* UN High Level Plenary Meeting on Financing for Development, Geneva.